The Marvellous Enchanted

Stephanie Marsden

BookLeaf Publishing

Presentation by *BookLeaf Publishing*

Web: www.bookleafpub.com

E-mail: info@bookleafpub.com

ISBN: 9789357616973

First edition 2022

Dedicated!

My father Steven.

*For always inspiring me out of the
goodness of his heart.*

PREFACE

Marvellous the Enchanted is a story poem written about love and compassion.
Feeling a connection with nature and the ones who wander along a river to the hidden forest making way to the desert.
Her name is Mae.
Depth is found within the abyss and found in knowledge within wisdom and try when you are prosperous and abundance is here. So that's what Mae did. Never boring always exploring and ideals begin to parade.

Natures Creatures

Once upon a time, our earth was blue, green and some parts yellow with mountains that sung opera that made the earthlings mellow.
Affirm through eventful days, living life safe and humble, I will see a brighter day. At a time liberation came so freely, to gain respect and your utter most
certainty.
I glared at a mushroom stool. I looked at the fungi and I said:
"Do, as you will for you are free, never feel lonely as you have me. It is moments like these in times to believe. Sun moves from behind the trees to help us see. Moon at full peak is ever the more visible as sun sets to darkness causing the inevitable. Energies to be heightened and emotions in full light cherished, I do believe is what makes you ever the more beautiful."
 I gravitate north as I shuffle my feet. Hip to the side I reside in rhythm and rhyme. Mountains and blue sky, even the moon has an eye. I could feel the jungle I looked over, dense. There was a green stem and a flower scent. The petal is lush. As I peered, the jungle said:

"The judgments you make on myself are one that is seen in the true self. Is it for help or is it for nurture? The true loss in life is loss of morals and integrity and the grace of your identity. Stay true to you. Keep your spirit high yet always humble. The only way you can be deterred from your true path is if you listen to the noise of the world and not from what's within your heart."

The Awakening

I walked to the river, stared at my reflection and spoke to the rock behind. Like a wall, a tall man appeared; ginger beard. Which way to follow me, so as I did..

As I am become overwhelmed I feel emotion, I begun to become aware of the world around me. I didn't even need to know where I'm going on this excursion. Before this tattooed man could peep. I begin to have strength behind what I speak. I start to chant strength behind the cry. "Down to the river to wash and drown my tears, refreshing my soul from spiral to reveres. Revealing what's inside, beauty in the connection to natures chimes. All in time. As cold is bearing on my skin, sensitive flesh is awakening. I Immerse myself into profound water.

Cooling my muscle, I see into the earth. As I look up to the misty forest I see heavenly trees heavily rooted to the ground. I dry my skin. I need to make a stance, so I start to dance. Shoulders back, head is high, all you ever need is I. Only self could walk along this trail that nature created for all to unveil."

Mother Nature Dream

Step by step, inch by inch, closer I become more
than
perceived image. My memory is at the core but
learning even more.
Feels like I'm living within a dream hazed by the
noise, yet complete, at peace
when it comes to poise. If I end with the
beginning, will I mend, love might become a
trend. I constantly lose myself to continuously
find myself.
Onwards and upwards. Shoot for the moon!
Earth is my guardian, the wind is my chimes,
water intuitively
creating the in-described. In time I'll find peace
in
human kind, until then I've got to work on mine.
Sadness doesn't last forever, sometimes madness
takes it toll. The feeling of keeping your head
held high when really you want to cry about it
all.. Love thy neighbor, love your family, love
those close to you. Yet, love yourself most
importantly. Life can bring you down but you'll
make your way back up. Life can be grand…
never forget how much life means to you.

Thrill that is Respected

In depth the stormy sky with clouds that
covered, about to cry.. thunder began, it was all
of a sudden, it was a touch frightening.
Adrenalin rushed through my veins, yet it all felt
so tame. I knew this was all to do with change.
  As the thunder develops, I see rocks standing
tall up a hill. I am on the ball. I search for a
cave. Leading to faith so I'm safe.

"A rainbow may appear after the storm."
A skipping leprechaun said.
"He's one of the ones richer ones, full of colour
and pride." I enthusiastically said.

As he skipped along so jolly, following him; a
trail of Molly.
Into the dark sky, he was able to still shine his
light. I began to become acquired to find my
desire with my heart and mind. I felt a flow of
ecstasy. Minerals and nutrients, I had saved
came flowing through my veins with a sudden
flare. I then decide to gain the courage to meet
my mentors and earn a legacy.

Then, as the storm disappeared and the sky was
clear; though I knew it wasn't for long, in search
of cover, I hummed my current favourite song.

Time is of the Essence, this is my greatest
lesson. I'm bold and I'm out here because I
don't fit the mold. I'd hoped to see a feather…
as a sign. As I seek my spirit guide, there's one
that comes to mind.
I saw him gaze at the scenery not far from me,
he noticed and started to walk towards me..

Glowing Sapphire

This I know! the man listening came forth and told 'your words mend.'
"Glowing sapphire is what they call me from the city I grew up in. I hope you meet your needs and acquire all you desire along your blessed sense."
Without a blink of an eye, I approach this handsome man with a grungy edge and tattoos, I explain how a woman like myself lived in a civilization, yet being who I am - there has always been an altercation.
So I begin to say with feeling and no hesitation..

As it goes a woman shows and has a lot to know.
In the greater scheme of the cosmos.
She finds empowerment in script, in the flow as it goes.
Many love of the young.
A child-like spirit of a girl, the best, she has one song that comes to mind.
Enhancing qualities, unique abilities. Give her one chance and it could be a billion opportunities.

As I know, I see there is a difference between
the knowers and the believers. Tell me if it's
similarities to the birds and the bees.
Not confusion…. Birds chirp and I'm the bees
knees. Yet really this is still the beginning, I said
gently. What else is out here, a rainforest
unsaid.

Here is one I kept tight it goes just like this, a
risk I take at night…
Karma is the universal flow, it's the biggest teller
of all.
No-one can play karma they must let it roll. If
they do, it may be an object of desire. I've
experienced first
hand and you know what the one playing karma
respectfully says so. What you say must be
thought out thoroughly with that being said your
actions are always higher.

Sophistication

As I spoke my truth I began to say:
You see when your minds a bit of a clutter
doesn't seem like much else matters.
Reconstructing ability and endurance creating
sophistication. Don't over share, beware. A
smile a day on the road to recovery is your
greatest discovery.
Converse query navigate narrate! Ask, and be
one with many; be merry. Take it slow; meaning
with each count and flow. Don't get to near.
You'll make proper sense talking from a
distance. Mind over matter, Everything is what
you make of it. Cultivated being to be admired.
I wouldn't be here without you and you
wouldn't be here without me. Don't you agree?

Hey there man with ginger beard. You've heard
me talk now say something… anything… even
if it's weird" so he began to say:

Structure will come tomorrow if you do good
today. You don't have to stay quiet if you have
nothing nice to say. Don't stay too far away,
you'll never know what you've started. Travel
near and far, The experience of life tells tales of

of revelation come to a tale yet be strengthened by the story of its creACTION. What will come from the equation. All abroad each has a line patters forming, we are all apart off love and compassion. Because when that happens reality kicks in to what really matters. Love is a win.

So once glowing sapphire reflects and illuminates he then begins to accumulate. Having my spiritual awakening discovering calm waters. When your young its mainly nonsense, when was it perfect to make sense. I stop and ponder and try to wonder. Tomorrow's a new day. You'll step forward on the trail of success.
Achieve then…. With solid foundations it never hurts to start again.

"Thanks mister, you've earnt this. I handed the man moonshine bottle. A pretty green and purple label.

Sister Ceremony

A raindrop fell on my cheek. Eep.. Better find
cover.
Standing on a cliff I began to lift my body into a
cave. "Thanks for to listen and for your wisdom"
I waved to the man with the ginger beard, who
really wasn't that weird.
It wasn't heavy rain. I just knew the rains were
on their way again.

Climb and climb I make my way through the
dim cave I won't know what's here till I….
Light a fire… walk away. As I toast my hands
on the fire I made.

I began the ceremony: As i listen to the rain pour
upon my roof i lay in bliss. To savor my energy i
am almost ready for the day to begin, one step
closer to igniting the goddess within. A play of
the flight, further more a ceremony of the fight.
Fight of our subconscious suppression of the
mind, body and soul. To serve our highest self of
what awaits behind every closed door. Rest our
spirit until freedom of our heart is herd. Regain
sisterhood and utter respect for our givings we

have served. All that is will be and all that has
been will be again.

Refuse to fall from Grace

A cosy toast a rug with a pillow. A bed made out
of willow.
My soul is fine, I've been divine, I'll arise again
and again like a phenix. I feel restless as though
there's something going on amongst us.

Evolution is the essence when I have insight.
Then it's enterprising surroundings. A
magnificent show. Bravo.

I thirst for love I cry for peace and I meditate,
turn off to turn on. I seek connection and
affection? when you meet people it's a
redirection. Steady pace you cant get lost when
you meet people who refuse to fall from grace
Hidden in the cave overnight.
Sleep tight.
Crackle pop (fire answered)
Hushhhhh.
REST
Be blessed don't overdo it. Overcome it.
Rest your head gently on your bed as you please
don't worry about what's been said.

Singular Fae

I arose darkness with a hint of burning coal.
I knew I was ready for the day to begin,
 I try to stand tall. Yet still bleak to see as the
cave is dark, I can feel the crystals.
I guide my way with energy,
In the cave bigger than me.
I'm yet a wanderer though believe this if you
May.
My balance kept me stable as I crawl on the
marble.
Out the other end, is my mission. To send a
message with your permission. I can speak to
animals and nature, humans and beings.
Psychically I knew the crystals in the cave took
me on another whirlwind this time I felt higher
and higher, it felt so strong I could see a fairy
she began to tell me about nature in her
perception and I could see her flying her dust
underlining. In my brain I could hear her say.

Wilderness it calls animals, dirt and trees. Nature
is speaking to palms, birds and leaves. So much
wisdom is hidden in Mother Nature. Be at peace
with the serenity no greater necessity than the
clarity and strength in the forest prosperity.

"Bye fairy" as she blessed me on her way. She
left in quite a hurry. I tried to stay still yet I
hope I didn't scare her away.

These crystals are giving me power!
Endurance is gold.
She's thoughtful, Silver is new and old.
I dream of the forest as the light peeps through.
Shine and twinkle. This cave is grand. How
many men has been here and haven't been
bland.
My ancestors I know are with me although I
travel on my own. Unravelling and challenging.
Really quite baffling. I begin another chant this
time it's spoken
Can I see through these shades. I think I use to
wear rose gold glasses. Yet when I remove them
I'm clear as day. It may be dark right now yet
when the sun rises brighter and riper.
It does get cold so I'll give you a piece of my
mind or I'll try buy some time.
Yet really I want to learn how to be the best in
this point in time. I want to learn to be there for
you but really I want to be here with you.
Is it because she's smart in the abyss, absolute
bliss. Yet drawn to bring attention to every
outcome as though a feather as a sign. Or a

butterfly for this point in time. Maybe it not
what you think, maybe it's the weather.
movements through improvements go for gold
make a song. It all started with the inspiration
and aspiration of where we began. Rhythm and
rhyme at what point in time do I put a drum to a
bass? How do I let the rain wash away my
problems let it reside let it clean inside in a
wider spectrum. Arising to the expectations of
how you can always do better.

I know I'm on the right path but there must be
something I have missed as find my way to exit
the cave.

Try and keep your cool and protection is not
affection. Be strong have courage.
Be subjective. After all it's about the Conception
of the idea of God and his honor.
Who will forgive him. How will we win.
Without sin. Is it going to be even?

Sunshine Daytime

As I began to see day, at a literal bright light at
the end of the tunnel I followed this light.
Then the sun appeared everything is clear.
I'm grounded and cleansed hoping to meet a
friend.
As I overlooked the fresh air and view of the
mountains as I reached the end of a cliff, coming
out to the forest. I said:

Sometimes I wonder do we think of the moon
during the day time? Or are we soaking in the
sun. Is a sun a star, our star, a sun star. Do we
call them stars because their far away? Do we
call it the sun because it brightens our lives
everyday.
Sunflower always facing the sun. Is there
another word for sun? Or is there none because
there's only one?

How has our atmosphere came to be was it
called
upon from rotations around the sun warming the
sea.
A magnetic rock and a ball of lava. It's all quite
Exquisite. Is GOD a wizard. that watches from a

moon beam? The last form of magic is art.
Nature is a mirror in which we study ourselves.
It's a reflection, is
there living spirit in a rainbows complexion.
As I send blessings from the earth to the moon
from the sea.

Ready to Meet the King

I see in the trees
A king sitting on a throne with a seat below.
"This is for the queen. You have within you. One
seat and you'll see your virtue. Im a blessed
king. To show Something when you've come
this far! Now tell me who you are?
I know you've been talking to beings along your
travel.
I've watched you so far along this trail. There's
a frequency that comes from the woods. I see
you choose your conversation and that's
something that won't fail. It's the wilderness and
because I see you creating innocence. Here's a
present to you.

You've been with the modern day yet now is
your time to gain excellence.
You've already recited the forest chant all the
way to the beach now I'm here to show you a
rainbow. If the challenge can be recited before
tomorrow.

Before you sit on the throne recite what you said
the very last day

I'll reveal to you everything you need regain a
form of success:a view, a manuscript please go
ahead. "
I began to say. "So the storm I hope I see a
rainbow"
He had begin to laugh. I know this is a blast
from the past before you knew the right rhythm
and rhyme yet you've been so good now tell us
how hard it was for you at first:"
So I began to chant:
I'm all eyes. I am able to see the hurt, mistrust
behind
the lies. I am able to see the defeat behind the
depth
of a wounded soldiers eyes. Suppression break
through to introspective. Careful enough to
reach the
limit. Living here is our greatest so live it.
Always
keep your hardest moments humble."

The cloud become a staircase I climbed on his
throne below.
The king turned into gold interchangeable; his
own. He showed me a script illuminate the
manuscript. recite with my imagination here's
what came from the equation:

Rainbow

Change is inevitable, without change there is no growth. It must alter our perspectives to change ways in love and light so you can use both. As change is growth our mind will expand. We can only grow greater its all in the plan.
As divine plan is heavens touch I hope you believe for its these angels who are holy its them that we need. Yet once were okay the angels leave. On the way to heaven so they leave us be. We will be send on the exploration and destination of discovery, self growth and recovery. One day its our turn once all has healed I hope I hold the decision to have the vision so I can be freed to plant the seed. Its for the ever growing consciousness and desire of my ego but I should mainly use my brain if I want to remain sane. I saw a rainbow today I think it was from the rain. Promise us one thing you'll never let your heart become plain.

Light waves of energy

I thought goodness what an adventure,
One more thing before before we head out I say
as mature as I can.
I believe in magic, I'm not crazy i just see the
world a little different to average misery. Use in
smiles, used in hugs, use in words and signs
from up above.
Just like that I'm on my own: what a magical
experience when I sat on the queens throne I
must do the king justice. He chose me so I began
to explained frequency.

I entered a field of flowers some blue, some
yellow and some even red purple was hard to
find yet the sky glistened light bearing lilac,
mauve and pink.
I had time so I explained vibration waves to the
bush of bees hiding in the trees:
Long wave sound wave: low vibration
Short sound wave: light vibration
Light vibration can travel through anything like
the speed of light.
Vibration meets light:
Sun sending different light wave what makes
colors bright.

Flower Color reflect from sun
Red: low energy
Light: secrets
Blue: high energy

Field Of Flowers

All along I spun in a circle… it felt good yet
then came a challenging hurdle.
A jump and a leap and then I AM ZEN.
Life started with being turned on then I wrote off
faster than my pen. Really I had a lot to share,
I've been in search of you everywhere. I find
grace and solidarity yet I seek, connection and
clarity. Will I find Holy Matrimony? I may be
the best enterprise you can find. I hope I see
heaven here again. Send blessings from nature to
the earth, amen.
The earth is very rich for us they say heaven is a
place on earth. Its for the very best of our kind
the good and the greatness to reside. I have pride
in the air and fresh water flows through my hair.
 I ignite fire within I have love for all and
everything. I'm not afraid to make it there or
dance a four step square.
 A triangle has three points and when aligned
with the greater good is fair.

Flower Crown Lady

It was a liberated rhyme one on time. Then a beautiful lady appeared wearing a flower crown.
Is she the one? Is she real?

She then begin to explain how her husband had left her and now she's Depressed as I get dressed, crown and suit to impress, tears shed. Do I have a friend to call or am I always on my own? Some things are better left unsaid, until you cross paths and find that the truth is right in front of you. When you look for the truth you look for what's right. Will I live up to expectations or is this the end of my sanity. It all started with vanity. Now it's hard to shape the morality and respect you receive from your fellow humanity. I feel heavy.... Just one more outburst of tears and I'll feel better.... Day of distress. I'm unimpressed and upset about what's been done and said. Will I live up to my full potential. I need to focus on hard work that's essential. Maybe then I'll come out the other end a brighter beacon with success and find the love I seek and find peace within my pinecone.

"I'm sorry lady. I said it sounds you need some rest. I point lady in the direction of a nice Cosy bed. As this beautiful lady is so sad I start to cheer her up!
I feel for you lady you speak from the heart. I'm here to listen yet before you rest, let me heal you and tell you my greatest lesson."

Alignment

All we remember, to come forth into motion and futuristic pattern rise from the surface. Pretty and light, bold and strong. Never forget the godly ego is never wrong. What is a godly ego you say, well it's real far away. solar plexus at the waist sun and our solar system all in place. Ego sits on the right also be align 7 chakras in a line. All that's left in plain sight is the mountains upon mountains and trees trees and to feel the breeze with the number 3.

Constellation

I continue my journey.
Detections, rotation magnetic alignment sun the right
bright; I release love. Higher with warmth.
Detecting my next move, navigating my senses
joyfully on my lonesome mission to attract the
wholesome.
STAR dust fills the galaxy, maybe it's from a
talent agency.
Is this all real or are we living in a simulation?
Smell real? Looks real?
I hear a shell… the sound of the ocean! oh wait..
it is real!

Scientist

I am a truth seeker give yourself credit!!!!
I chant and as I beg a scientist hatched from an egg.
He had thick magnifying glasses that made his eyes pop!
"Tell me scientist how did you hatch from that egg?"

Beat chaos be progressive not aggressive. Alignment comes in many forms a newly awakened soul is still in its raw form. Watching from a spectrum is your soul. Stillness under the observation of your mind indicates frequency known as vibration. A steady particle withholds strength no matter the size. Forming a collective spectrum of light. Lifting all that is beneath into hindsight. Creation… revering… sensation. Learning the observational state initiating all surrounding, in the making action. Gravity to keep in touch with attraction.

Gods Blessing

This is where I stand.
 I begin to recite the script I remember from the gods.
I say god is always with me. In Jesus name amen.
all I can recite is the greatness held in the torch, as I held the light.

Gods will is his hopes and prayers, your hopes and prayers will appear with blessings. By practicing prayer your path may lead to the holy gates.

Mans judgment is a consequence of their actions ultimately what is said and done, and the karmic reaction that comes from these actions.
What man manifest will be ultimate to if the shall rise or fall.

Divine plan is beyond all A collective consciousness. It's seeing, believing, connecting, observing. Doing everything for the greater good.

Creation is god! To connect with your high level of being. Heaven is a place on earth yet heaven is to not loose your connection with the earth. Maybe it's not about following the religion it's about your relationship with god. Maybe it's about bringing a spiritual awakening with god and may your life grow.

Peace of Mind

Love will concur your fight and you will win
peace of mind

Thrive, bee hive. Unbelievable mind.

One of a kind. Planet earth thrive. Strive don't
fall behind. Is it the ever growing consciousness
that sends blessings from the earth to the moon
from the sea.
Be the light and understand love is unique. Love
is one and light is all.
Have an effect on those who show you how to
get along. So you can be the best alone or better
yet being at peace with this masterpiece.

I see a bird circling above he eggs me on. I see
more one by one…. is the scientist with the
bird… I'm unsure?
Yet I was egged on by the bird circling above so
I say to him as he does.
 so freely and smoothly:

"Be' is a nice word you see. To be and be there.
When you be you are free. You want to use it in
a

positive term. For it's the futuristic word that helps

you learn, past and present so you stay stern. Be gives strength in wanting some positive foundation

and the length of endeavors to be here and be there the

beach has a sea. I wouldn't be here without you and

you wouldn't be here without me... Don't you agree?

The planets align to a Goddess

An astrologer came forth behind a misty light
post. Appeared....
the whole universe.
"I heard you talk before I saw you lerk"
I said to the reader. The reader spoke of the
greatest love and
compassion.
She said to me:
Mars dig deep here, with your wisdom and dare
to build
character in this mission;
This she Admires the sun.
There comes a day most days we reach for the
rising star.
Yet you must be acquired with Venus desire.
Astro belt full of wonder with more gold
withheld than any
human on earth could ever get too prior.
Saturn the teller of the story, it's all she felt and
more so not
corny.
Not far from Uranus will you rate.
I'll be sure to see Jupiter. All she felt from you
and her. Just like

that she's back where she knew she would be.
Mercury, try now negotiate what is hired and
what you thrive.
How about that Neptune dream of how the
repressed
conscious minds vents.
-then there is Pluto in all its small and mighty
powerful The
power of the collective mini planets.
The earth is a living garden.

Here's the pun there's always time for fun, be
the light and understand love is unique. Love is
one and light is all.
This can be reversed at night now try and think
how?

Have an effect on those who show you how to
get along. So you can be the best alone or better
yet being at peace this masterpiece.
Mars got the car and we're far from the
constellation but basically square One with the
sun ☀

To be the best you must know better. To be all
you need you must have the courage to utilize
and lead.

Ahhhh, this journey is coming to an end I see
my car…. Then I see the man and boy walking
to the sunset.
An owl landed on a branch near my car. so I let
out a marvelous meaning, one that I should have
said from the beginning:

As we find faith in what is right, don't be afraid
to step
forward and shine your light. Solidarity and
youth
walk hand in hand into shared teachings and
times to
understand. To foresee what could be a better
outcome for the young. In all we see, pray for
strength in our inner child and all to succumb.
protector, man and boy, safely making their way
further, higher grounds for boy. For what was
prior
old is noble, young is able as time is in favor.
feeling in moments of bliss is what we search
and strive to
not miss. boy walks in hand with the old man
inheriting purity, love and strength to rise above.

One last thing for myself:
I lead through faith so I'm safe.

I get in my car and stare on the road. A magical
mystical journey. As I drive follow the lines..
 What comes to mind is a goddess who worships
time. What she said eases my mind:

Beautiful mind comes a beautiful life exquisite
sight behold the light goddess of time. A
moment you cherish sing of many love the good
and the strong sing it in song. To face the
greatness you must go through the greatest.

The end